COUNTRIES OF THE WORLD

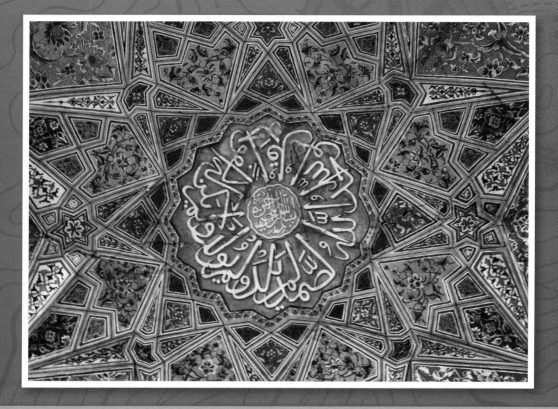

Assalam-o-Alaikum,
PAKISTAN

by Leah Kaminski

T0053971

CHERRY LAKE PUBLISHING • ANN ARBOR, MICHIGAN

Published in the United States of America by Cherry Lake Publishing
Ann Arbor, Michigan
www.cherrylakepublishing.com

Reading Adviser: Marla Conn MS, Ed., Literacy specialist, Read-Ability, Inc.

Book Design: Book Buddy Media

Photo Credits: ©hansslegers/Getty Images, cover (top), ©Amir Mukhtar/Getty Images, cover (bottom), ©commoner28th/Getty Images, 1, ©Steve Allen/Shutterstock, 3, ©Punnawit Suwuttananun/Getty Images, 4, ©Muhammad Farooq/500px/Getty Images, 5, ©Globe Turner, LLC/Getty Images, 6, ©Tahreer Photography/Getty Images, 7, ©Amir Mukhtar/Getty Images, 8, ©Brad Jackson/Getty Images, 9 (top), ©Visual News Pakistan/Getty Images, 9 (bottom), ©Nadeem Khawar/Getty Images, 10, ©S.M.Ali/PPI Photo/Newscom, 11, ©JackF/Getty Images, 12, ©Pardeep Singh Gill/Getty Images, 13, ©Juanmonino/Getty Images, 14, ©Bashir Osman's Photography/Getty Images, 15, ©ElasticComputeFarm/Pixabay, 16, ©Daniel Berehulak/Getty Images, 17, ©Daniel Berehulak/Getty Images, 18, ©Warrick Page/Getty Images, 19, ©Paula Bronstein/Getty Images, 20, ©Umar Qayyum/Xinhua/Newscom, 21, ©PPI/ZUMA Wire/Newscom, 22, ©Bashir Osman's Photography/Getty Images, 23 (left), ©Juanmonino/Getty Images, 23 (right), ©commoner28th/Getty Images, 24, ©Nabeel Ishaq/EyeEm/Getty Images, 25, ©Stefan Trappe/Caro/Newscom, 26, ©luxG4/Getty Images, 27, ©nazar_ab/Getty Images, 28, ©Bashir Osman's Photography/Getty Images, 29, ©Iqbal Khatri/Getty Images, 30, ©Aliraza Khatri's Photography/Getty Images, 31 (top), ©Monica Schipper/Getty Images, 31 (bottom), ©Photography By Waheed/Getty Images, 32, ©BM Photography/Getty Images, 33, ©jharris1124/Pixabay, 34 (top), ©jharris1124/Pixabay, 34 (bottom), ©Iqbal Khatri/Getty Images, 35, ©Bashir Osman's Photography/Getty Images, 36, ©Loyseau Benjamin/SIPA/Newscom, 37, ©ahmet_ozgur/Getty Images, 38, ©Jan Kruger/Getty Images, 39, ©SM Rafiq Photography./Getty Images, 40, ©Tahreer Photography/Getty Images, 41 (top), ©Tahreer Photography/Getty Images, 41 (bottom), ©Bashir Osman's Photography/Getty Images, 43, ©Amir Mukhtar/Getty Images, 44, ©Sisoje/Getty Images, 45, ©filo/Getty Images, background

Library of Congress Cataloging-in-Publication Data has been filed and is available at catalog.loc.gov

Cherry Lake Publishing would like to acknowledge the work of The Partnership for 21st Century Learning.
Please visit www.p21.org for more information.

Printed in the United States of America

TABLE OF CONTENTS

CHAPTER 1

WELCOME TO PAKISTAN!

The Passu Cathedral is a set of mountain peaks that tower more than 20,000 feet (6,000 meters) over northern Pakistan.

The **Islamic** Republic of Pakistan is located in South Asia. About twice the size of California, Pakistan has more than 207 million residents. This is the sixth-largest population in the world. Pakistan's Muslim population is the second-largest in the world.

Pakistan is known for its mix of ancient South Asian cultures. Beautiful Islamic art and architecture fill its cities, and its people enjoy traditional folk music and dance. The country's landscapes are rugged and beautiful. There are high mountains in the north, vast deserts, and beaches on the Arabian Sea at its southern borders.

The spotted owlet is one of many owl species found in Pakistan.

ACTIVITY

Look at the map of Pakistan and its surrounding neighbors. Using a separate sheet of paper, trace Pakistan. Follow the dotted lines that divide Pakistan into each of the **provinces** and the Federally Administered Tribal Areas (FATA). Using the information in this chapter, and having an adult help you look online if necessary, label each area.

More than 50 million acres (20 million hectares) of land is used for farming in Pakistan.

Pakistan is bordered by Afghanistan and Iran to the west, China to the north, and India to the east. Most of Pakistan's land is filled with mountains and high plateaus. The huge Indus River plain takes up much of the country. Most of Pakistan's land is divided into four provinces. These are Sindh, Punjab, Khyber Pakhtunkhwa, and Balochistan.

Sindh is in the south. Sindh's capital, Karāchi, is Pakistan's largest and most diverse city. Karāchi is also the country's main seaport. Balochistan, next to Iran, is Pakistan's largest province, but is the least populated. It is very dry.

Punjab, in the east, is Pakistan's most populated and wealthy area. It has many farms along the Indus River. Punjab's capital is Lahore, where the country's films are made. Pakistan's capital, Islamabad, is also in Punjab. Islamabad was a planned city built in the 1960s.

The Abbassi Royal Graveyard houses the graves of the Abbassi family in the Punjab region of Pakistan.

Severe storms and difficult terrain makes K2 one of the world's most dangerous mountains to climb.

Khyber Pakhtunkhwa in the north is Pakistan's most mountainous area. It is home to K2, the world's second-highest peak. K2 is 28,251 feet (8,611 m) above sea level. There are also some areas of Pakistan that are outside of the provinces. For example, to the southwest of Khyber Pakhtunkhwa is a region called the Federally Administered Tribal Areas, or FATA.

Deadly Waters

Pakistan has experienced severe flooding in the past decade. Around 2,000 people died when the Indus River flooded in 2010, and hundreds more have died in floods since then. The flooding is likely an effect of climate change. Pakistan does not create many carbon emissions because it is a poor country. However, Pakistan still feels the effects of climate change.

Pakistan's climate varies from frozen mountaintops to hot beaches. But the entire country is very dry. The large provinces of Sindh and Balochistan in the south, as well as much of Punjab, receive less than 10 inches (25 centimeters) of rain per year.

Most of Pakistan has three different seasons. The hot season runs from March through June. The wet season, also called the monsoon, lasts from July through September. The cold season runs from October through February.

In rural parts of Punjab, houses are made of mud. The mud naturally keeps homes cool in summer and warm in winter.

The Indus River Dolphin

The Indus River dolphin, a freshwater dolphin, is one of the world's rarest mammals. The condition of the Indus River dolphin population is a sign of the overall health of the Indus River and surrounding land. It is the second-most endangered freshwater dolphin species. Its habitat has been damaged by fishing, pollution, and dams.

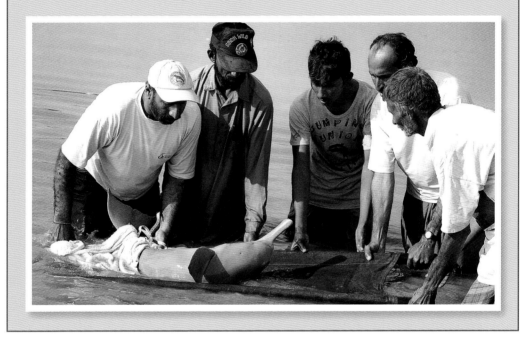

High elevations in the north often dip below freezing. Plain regions can reach up to 117 degrees Fahrenheit (47 degrees Celsius) in the summer. It can be so hot that trees shed leaves to avoid losing more moisture through their leaf surfaces.

The wet season in Pakistan is not very wet compared to other countries that have monsoon seasons. In addition, because monsoon rains come during the hot summer, a lot of the moisture is **evaporated** in the heat.

Pakistan naturally has very little forest. This is because of its deserts and high mountains. Markhor goats live in the cold mountains of Pakistan. These wild goats with spiral horns are Pakistan's national animal. Snow leopards also live in the mountains. They are one of Pakistan's most endangered animals.

A male markhor's horns can grow to be 5 feet (1.5 m) long!

CHAPTER 2

BUSINESS AND GOVERNMENT IN PAKISTAN

The country of Pakistan has a complicated history. Pakistan, present-day India, and Bangladesh were all colonized by the British in the 1800s. They were called British India.

India and Pakistan became independent republics in 1947. Pakistan was separated into the East and the West. Pakistan was meant for Muslims, and India was meant for Hindus. This was called the Partition of India, and its purpose was to keep the peace. But at first, it did the opposite. Muslims in India and Hindus in Pakistan were beaten, killed, and driven out. More than 1 million people died.

The border between India and Pakistan is monitored by security patrols.

There are almost 2 billion Muslims around the world.

In the first years of independence, millions of Muslims fled to Pakistan, and millions of Hindus and Sikhs fled to India. Overall, it is estimated that nearly 15 million people were displaced in the following decades. Pakistan's borders continued to change. For example, India and Pakistan have fought over Kashmir three separate times. Many people died in these conflicts.

A civil war broke out in 1971 between East and West Pakistan. The East's **indigenous** Bengali population, with the help of India, declared itself independent from the West. East Pakistan became Bangladesh.

Mohammed Ali Jinnah's remains are held within the Mazar-e-Quaid mausoleum in Karāchi.

Mohammed Ali Jinnah

Mohammed Ali Jinnah was Pakistan's first governor-general. Jinnah is considered Pakistan's founding father and held the title of Qaid-i-Azam, or "Great Leader." Jinnah worked hard to encourage peace during the fighting that followed independence.

ACTIVITY

Research the civilizations that have made Pakistan what it is today. Pakistan is the site of the Indus Valley Civilization, one of the oldest civilizations in the world. During the second millennium BCE, the Indo-Aryan people arrived. Other cultures have invaded Pakistan across the centuries, including the Persians, Greeks, and Turks, along with the Mughal and British Empires. They have all left their mark on this nation.

First, choose a culture to research. Then, narrow down your search with questions. Some questions you might ask are: Where did this culture come from? Why did they come to Pakistan? How did they enter Pakistan, peacefully or by force? What effect did they have on Pakistan? Can we see any of these effects today? The final step for good research is choosing the right sources for your answers. Ask your librarian to help you find information on your chosen culture in a book or online.

An estimated 50 percent of people in Pakistan participated in the 2018 election.

The 2018 Election

Pakistan's 2018 election was historic. There were deadly suicide bombings around voting places, but millions of Pakistanis voted. Women voted in large numbers for the first time. However, there is evidence that the military influenced the election to help Prime Minister Imran Khan and his party, Pakistan Tehreek-e-Insaf (PTI). PTI says it will help the poor and make Pakistan fair for people of all incomes and religions.

Today, Pakistan is led by a president, prime minister, and **parliament**. The people elect the president. The prime minister is elected by the parliament, which is called the National Assembly. They share power, but the president can dismiss the prime minister. In 2013, a **democratically elected** government transitioned power to another democratically elected government for the first time. In 2018, Imran Khan was elected prime minister and Arif Alvi was elected president.

Imran Khan focused his campaign on reducing corruption in the Pakistani government.

The large Badshahi Mosque in Lahore has room for 100,000 worshippers.

The religion of Islam is part of the Pakistani government. For example, the president and prime minister have to be Muslim. The Parliament is not allowed to make laws that go against Islam. There are also separate Islamic or Sharia law courts for personal issues.

Child Labor

Up to 13 million Pakistani children work. They make up a large percentage of the country's workers. They often work in physically difficult jobs, for no money or pennies a day. The Pakistani government has worked to improve these issues. Poor parents receive money so that their children will not have to work. In 2017, anti–child labor laws in Sindh were made stronger.

More than 4 million people were left without homes after a 2005 earthquake outside Muzaffarabad, Pakistan.

Pakistan has struggled to build up its economy. One cause of its economic difficulties is that the government has not been stable. Safety concerns from terrorist groups such as Al-Qaeda and the Taliban also prevent the country from thriving. These groups take advantage of poverty to control rural regions and base their terrorist operations there. Climate change, poor **infrastructure**, electricity shortages, and natural disasters are also reasons for Pakistan's struggles.

It is thought that up to 40 percent of Pakistanis live in poverty. Poverty involves more than not having money. It involves a person's ability to access what he or she needs to live. In Pakistan, the poor often do not have access to housing, utilities, education, medical care, and clean water.

Most of the children living in Pakistan's slums do not attend school.

CHAPTER 3

MEET THE PEOPLE

Many Pakistani cargo trucks, called "jingle trucks," are decorated with colorful paint, bells, and other adornments.

Two-fifths of Pakistanis farm and raise livestock. Pakistan has one of the largest **irrigation** systems in the world. Canals bring water from the Indus River to farm fields of wheat and sugarcane. The percentage of poverty has dropped since the turn of the 21st century. Improvement is slow, but the work continues.

Pakistan does not trade very much with other countries. Textiles are its biggest exports. Textile mills make cloth from cotton, silk, and **jute**.

Pakistan's population is almost 208 million. Several ethnicities call Pakistan home. Most of these ethnic groups live in specific provinces.

About half of Pakistanis are Punjabi. Many Punjabis work as farmers in the Indus Valley. The government and military are also composed of many Punjabis. Sindhis mainly live in the rural areas of Sindh. Pashtuns work as herders, farmers, and traders. They have a tribal system. Balochis in Balochistan are nomadic. Muhajirs are the **refugees** who fled to Pakistan during the partition in 1947 and 1948. Most settled in cities.

The southern province of Sindh is known for ornate embroidery and stitching.

The traditional blue burqa is popular among women in Pakistan.

Global refugee agencies provide support to Afghans living in Pakistan, including helping children continue their education.

There are also up to 2 million Afghan refugees in Pakistan. Refugees began leaving Afghanistan in 1979, fleeing Soviet military action. Since then, they have continued to enter Pakistan because of unrest in their country, such as the U.S. war against terrorist groups in Afghanistan. There is controversy over refugee rights. For example, there has recently been debate about whether refugee children born in Pakistan should be Pakistani citizens.

Pakistan is set apart from India by its large Muslim population. Muslims make up 96 percent of Pakistan's population. The Qur'ān is Islam's book of religious teachings. It encourages its followers to live pure religious lives and be charitable. Mosques are where followers of Islam pray. They are often very beautiful. Pakistan has many beautiful and ancient mosques, such as the Pearl Mosque and Badshahi Mosque.

The Badshahi Mosque and Pearl Mosque were built in the 1600s.

Marriage and family is one of the most important parts of life as a Muslim.

Islamic tradition also directs family life. Several generations of a family live together under the same roof. The oldest man in the family is the head. Women are seen as secondary. They run the household and raise the children.

Many families practice purdah. Purdah is the Muslim practice of keeping women from being seen by men. Women's zones of the house are separated from men's zones. When a woman goes outside, she covers her head or wears a burqa. A burqa cloaks her entire body, including her face. Some wealthy women and those who live in cities do not practice purdah.

While many women are pressured to cover themselves, others choose to wear a burqa for religious, cultural, or fashion reasons.

The national language of Pakistan is Urdu. Most Pakistanis understand and speak Urdu. Business is often done in English. English is one of the country's official languages, and around half of Pakistanis speak English. Around 70 languages are spoken in Pakistan. Most are tied to a region or ethnicity, such as Punjabi or Sindhi. Almost half of the country speaks Punjabi as its first language.

An estimated 100 million people speak Urdu in Pakistan, India, and other nearby countries.

ACTIVITY

Through its history, Urdu has traded words and phrases with other
languages. These have included Persian, Arabic, Hindi, and English. The
Urdu words below have either been influenced by the English language
or adopted into English in some form. Can you guess what each word
means? See below for the answers.

1. *plet*

2. *machiz*

3. *pyjama*

4. *dactr*

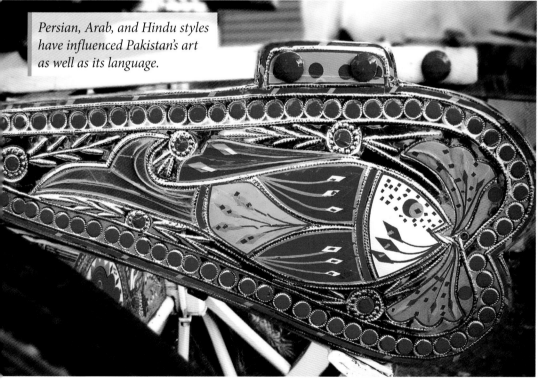

Persian, Arab, and Hindu styles
have influenced Pakistan's art
as well as its language.

(plate, matches, pajamas, doctor)

While many rural areas of Pakistan have schools for young children, there are few opportunities for them to attend high school or college.

About 44 percent of school-age Pakistani children did not attend school in 2015 and 2016. Pakistan has the second worst out-of-school rate in the world.

There are many reasons for this problem. Some students work in factories. In rural areas, schools may be far away or have no electricity. Many families keep girls home. Some Pakistanis do not believe in educating women. Also, girls are not always safe walking to school.

There is work being done to solve this. The government gives money to families to send girls to school. Low-cost private schools are also becoming popular.

Frere Hall was built in the 1860s to be the town hall of Karāchi. It now serves as a library.

Malala Yousafzai

A 21-year-old Oxford University student, Malala Yousafzai is also an international activist for women's education. In 2014, she became the youngest Nobel Peace Prize winner. Malala grew up in Khyber Pakhtunkhwa, where the Taliban stopped girls from receiving education. The Taliban shot her when she was 15 because of her activism. This attack only caused her to work harder.

CHAPTER 4

CELEBRATIONS

Pakistanis love poetry and music. Poetry readings, called *mushairas*, are a popular form of entertainment. Pakistani poetry is often about romantic love and love for God. Politics and the plight of the poor are common too.

Poems are often set to music. *Qawwali* poetry uses lyrics from religious poetry. *Ghazals* are another poetry form often set to music. Sometimes these songs become lyrics for pop music. Besides Pakistani pop and Western pop, Pakistani radio plays classical Pakistani songs called ragas. *Filmi* songs, based on Indian and Pakistani films, are also very popular.

Pakistani folk singers are often accompanied by drums, sitars, or flutes.

Many marriages in Pakistan are arranged, which means the bride and groom are chosen by their families or community.

One place to hear wonderful music is at a wedding ceremony. At a traditional Pakistani wedding, the ceremony is conducted outside under a large tent. A *quazi*, or religious leader, performs the ceremony.

ACTIVITY

Before a Pakistani wedding, the bride's hands and feet are painted in decorative patterns with henna paste. Henna paste is a reddish dye. Below are two designs. On a separate sheet of paper, try drawing the designs yourself. The patterns are detailed. Using a thin colored pencil for your sketches will work best.

A bride's henna art includes many symbols for love, luck, and sometimes the name of the groom.

Islam has two major celebrations, or *eids*, during the year. One is called Eid al-Fitr. It marks the end of Ramadan, the month of fasting. During this month, Muslims don't eat or drink from dawn until sunset. The act of fasting is said to redirect attention from worldly activities and cleanse the soul. It also allows Muslims to practice sympathy for those who are less fortunate. Eid al-Fitr falls after this month of fasting. On the first morning of the celebration, everybody goes for special prayers. Children receive gifts and money. There are fairs with music, dancing, and games.

Street markets are busy before big festivals in Pakistan, as people buy special outfits, decorations, and gifts for the holidays.

Pop Culture in Pakistan

Pakistan has a huge pop music scene. The music is popular around the world. Currently popular are singers such as Meesha Shafi and Sajjad Ali and bands such as Garam Anday. With its feminist lyrics, Garam Anday's catchy 2018 song *"Maan Behn Ka Danda"* is one of many new political songs in Pakistani pop.

Meesha Shafi is a successful model, actress, and singer.

Only healthy sheep that are at least 1 year old are chosen for Eid al-Adha.

Islam's other major holiday is called Eid al-Adha. This *eid* celebrates the story of the prophet Abraham. To prove his love, Abraham was willing to sacrifice his son, Ishmael, to God. God stopped him at the last minute and had him kill a lamb instead. During Eid al-Adha, an animal is slaughtered to remember this story. One-third of the meat is given to the poor, one-third to friends, and one-third to family. Gifts and meals are part of the celebration too.

Cricket

Some of the world's best cricket players have come from Pakistan. Prime Minister Imran Khan is one of the greatest Pakistani cricketers ever. More recent greats are Younis Khan and Mohammad Yousuf. In 1992, Pakistan won the Cricket World Cup. This event is considered the most important cricket competition in the world.

CHAPTER 5

WHAT'S FOR DINNER?

Most Pakistanis eat three meals each day. Breakfast is the lightest meal. Dinner features many dishes served all at one time. People eat dinner as late as 9 p.m. Visitors who stop by are always invited to share with their hosts.

Pakistanis usually eat with their hands, sometimes scooping food with flatbreads such as *roti* and *chapati*. They always use the right hand. The left hand is reserved for tasks such as taking off shoes.

Lea Market in Karāchi includes vendors of fresh fruit, vegetables, meat, fish, and milk.

Rice with kebabs, meat that is marinated and grilled, is a common meal in Pakistan.

Little cake-like sweets are Pakistani favorites for parties and celebrations.

Pakistani **cuisine** varies by ethnicity and region. Overall, it is similar to Indian food. Curry dishes are common, using vegetables such as potatoes, lentils, eggplant, and okra and meats such as beef, chicken, and mutton. Yogurt is a common ingredient. Muslim Pakistanis never eat pork because it is considered unclean.

RECIPE

Mithi roti is a type of sweet flatbread. You can eat it for breakfast or as a snack. This recipe requires using a stovetop and working with hot oil. Be sure to have an adult help. Here's what you'll need:

INGREDIENTS:

2 cups (256 grams) whole wheat flour, plus more for kneading and rolling (you could also use chapati flour)

1 tablespoon (6 g) brown sugar

warm water

2 to 3 tablespoons (30 to 44 milliliters) vegetable oil

INSTRUCTIONS:

1. Combine the flour and water into a bowl. Start with 2/3 cup (158.5 ml) water. Add slightly more water if the dough is too dry. Add more flour if the dough is too sticky.

2. Knead well until you have a tender mass of dough. Let it sit for approximately 15 minutes.

3. Take a glob of dough that is slightly larger than a golf ball. Work it into a ball.

4. Flour the rolling pin and your work surface. Using the pin, roll the dough into a flat circle.

5. Use a pastry brush to evenly spread a layer of oil over the surface of the dough.

6. Start at one edge of the dough. Using your fingers, roll up the dough into a tube, from one edge all the way to the opposite edge. Next, work this tube of dough into a coil, almost like a cinnamon bun.

7. Use your palm to press the dough flat. Roll it out with the rolling pin. Have an adult heat 1 tablespoon (15 ml) of oil in a pan.

9. Once the oil is warm, carefully lay the *roti* dough in the pan.

10. After 1 minute, add another layer of oil and a sprinkling of brown sugar on top of the *roti*. Spread evenly with the pastry brush. Use a spatula to carefully flip the *roti* over.

11. The bread is finished when both sides are golden brown.

12. Repeat step #3 through step #10 until you've used all the dough.

Enjoy!

Flatbreads like mithi roti do not include yeast or other ingredients that make bread rise, or get fluffy.

Pakistanis eat many interesting desserts. *Jalebis* are one example. They consist of a deep-fried batter dunked in sticky sugar syrup. Pakistanis cool off with a version of ice cream called *kulfi*. Lassi, a cold, yogurt-based drink, is similar to a smoothie. Common flavors are honey, cinnamon, mint, mango, and banana.

Pakistanis also drink hot tea, which they call chai. It is a part of how they welcome guests. Perhaps you will visit a Pakistani house one day!

Tea is an important part of Pakistani culture. Different types are traditional to ethnic groups across the country.

The Spice of Pakistan

A lot of Pakistani dishes are seasoned with masala. Masalas are special blends of spices. Families often have their own favorite masala recipe.

GLOSSARY

cuisine *(kwih-ZEEN)* a style of cooking, usually associated with a certain country or region

democratically elected *(de-muh-KRA-tik-lee i-LEK-ted)* put into office by the vote of the common people

evaporated *(i-VA-puh-ray-ted)* changed from a liquid into a gas

indigenous *(en-DIJ-en-uhs)* people native to a specific area

infrastructure *(IN-fruh-struhk-chur)* the basic equipment and systems of a place, such as bridges, roads, and power

irrigation *(ihr-uh-GAY-shuhn)* the process of moving water in order to use it for agriculture

Islamic *(iss-LAHM-ik)* having to do with the culture and religion of Muslims, who believe in one God, Allah, and his prophet, Muhammad

jute *(JOOT)* a natural fiber made from plants that is used to make rope and rough cloth

parliament *(PAHR-luh-ment)* in certain types of government, the group of people responsible for creating laws

provinces *(PROV-in-sihz)* large parts of a country

refugees *(REF-yoo-jeez)* people who are forced to flee their homelands and live in other countries

FOR MORE INFORMATION

BOOKS

Abouraya, Karen Leggett. *Malala Yousafzai: Warrior with Words.* New York: Lee & Low Books Inc., 2018.

Khan, Hena. *Night of the Moon: A Muslim Holiday Story.* San Francisco: Chronicle Books, 2018.

Marsico, Katie. *Islam.* Global Citizens: World Religions. Ann Arbor, MI.: Cherry Lake Publishing, 2017.

WEB SITES

National Geographic—Pakistan's Most Wild and Beautiful Places
https://www.nationalgeographic.com/travel/destinations/asia/pakistan/beautiful-natural-wonders
See more of Pakistan's natural beauties with photos and information by National Geographic.

Oddizzi—Pakistan
https://www.oddizzi.com/teachers/explore-the-world/places/asia/pakistan
Read about the famous people, popular food, and animals of Pakistan.

United Religions Initiative—Islam: Basic Beliefs
https://www.uri.org/kids/world-religions/muslim-beliefs
Explore the history, basic beliefs of Islam, with links to Musilim imagery, sacred spaces, and more.

INDEX

ABOUT THE AUTHOR

Leah Kaminski loves international travel. She especially likes learning about the culture and ecology of other countries. Leah lives with her husband and baby boy in Chicago, where she teaches, writes poetry, and writes books like this one.